BEAUTY
FOR
ASHES

BEAUTY
FOR
ASHES

By
Zy'Kia Newby

TUCKER
PUBLISHING HOUSE LLC

"To console those who mourn in Zion, To give them beauty for ashes, The oil of joy for mourning, The garment of praise for the spirit of heaviness; That they may be called trees of righteousness, The planting of the LORD, that He may be glorified.""

Isaiah 61:3 NKJV

Table of Contents

Like spring dew to new leaves or a freshly cut rose to one's lover, here is my ode to you. My dear healing processes. And to the one I love the most, my heavenly Father. May these poems help all who come across them to grow in the Love of God, the faithfulness of Jesus Christ, and the fruits of the Holy Spirit. Peace and Love be to you all. May Jehovah Sholom's watchful Eyes, careful Hands, and loving Heart be with you always.

Shalom Shalom.

Brown Skin

• • •

My beautiful melanin has been so sweet to me,
It is a treat to be in this cocoa butter scented skin.

God thought of Himself when He made me,
So, whatever the case may be,
Being a beautiful Brown lady
I love it here.

Though it is dangerous
I am dangerously in love with you.
The way you dance with both the sun and the Son.
Walk amongst the stars,
And electric slide with the moonlight

But I must also remember,
You are fragile, like the most pristine piece of art,
So, I must be careful with you.
Careful to clarify that you are not bulletproof.
Nor fireproof
But in this white America

It seems to me that they see you as hire proof.
And themselves as liar proof.

But you are NOT who they say you are,
My beautiful shining star.
You are elegant,
You are pristine,
You are made in the image of God.
You are…. Perfect
For He Himself created you and said,
"It is good."

So don't you ever forget that you descended from not
only Kings and Queens,
but from the Lord Himself, the Divine Creator.

Don't let these babbling fools,
and blaspheming haters tell you any less than who
God says you are!
You are one of my brightest stars, my beautiful brown
skin.

~ Z.

Emotional

"Why are you so emotional?" They said.

I dread that I felt dead on the inside,
My insides slowly decaying away.
I've been trying to stray away and stay away,

From that adjective

Emotional

As I fight tears from all these years
Of abuse and neglect, beaten when I object.
Having always been left to wonder,
"What's next?"
As I regret even uttering a word about my pain
Left in anguish over my brokenness.

Why can't I fix it?

Why was I born?

Why am I here, hurting everyone so
near and dear to me?

Why is everything my fault?

Why do the kids at school hate me?
Why doesn't anyone wanna date me,
Why do I feel...so... alone?

And again, they said,

"Why are you so emotional?"

~ Z.

7777

7 wishes
7 wonders
7 wanders
7 hungers

7 wishes for the days of our youth.
7 wonders for revelation from the Truth.
7 wanders into a land flowing with milk and honey.
7 hungers for a world driven more by love and less by
greed and money.

7 years
7 months
7 days
7 hours and minutes

All will be love, wars will cease, evil will vanish, and
peace will increase.

~ Z.

Healing

Healing to break the sealing,
of this pain that I'm feeling.

God willing, I was able to silence the wailing.
Caused by the ailments of my past.

Then there was beauty and joy
Peace and love from above.

And dare I say, I feel free at last.

Free at last.

~ Z.

Little Bird

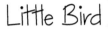

Marching to the beat of the drums of God
My sweet Little Bird
Unheard of amongst the masses
A controversial existence.

From the land up above,
Flowing with milk and honey
Living in a world teeming with sorrows and money
My Little Bird
Please understand me,
Because they will never understand you.

Fight and fuss, tooth, and nail
Run into the streets, shout and flail.
The Messiah is coming.
But they will not hear you.

They will see you in the bustling streets and strut
right past you.

My dear Little Bird,
Please understand me,
Because they will never understand you.

"He will cover you with his feathers. He will shelter
you with his wings. His faithful promises are your
armor and protection.
Do not be afraid of the terror by night,
Nor of the arrows that fly by day,
Nor of those who walk in darkness,
Nor of the destruction that lays waste at noonday."
(Psalm 91:4-6)

For many shall run to and fro, but the end is not yet.
So do not fear Little Bird.
The end will be peace and love,
Joy without pain
Sunshine with rain
And Love without end.

Please understand me Little Bird,
Because few will ever understand you.

~ Z.

I Won't Fit

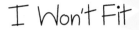

I won't fit.
I refuse to be ripped to pieces, bit by bit,
Because I don't fit.
Because I won't fit, because that. wont. fit.
I am tired of having to live up to the lies of other
people's lives that aren't mine because of the knives
that were put into their backs.

Because of their lack, I suffer, but
What God has put together,
let no man (or woman) put asunder.

I refuse to be under restrictions and restraints of who
I am or what I ain't.
I'm not an idiot,
because I wouldn't stitch the pieces that you handed.

Re-fly the plane that you landed,
Or re-sing the song that you demanded.

I am me now, and you can't change that.

What you broke, God has to rearrange that and put
her back together.
The many nights I cried, "Jesus please help me"
because of what YOU did.

He had to put my broken pieces back together due to
the constant policing that you did.

"What to wear and what not to wear."
"What to say and what not to say."
Well, no thanks, that's not ok!
The constant day to day replay of what I did
or didn't do, because within you, it won't click.

That "you crazy" or "you do too much"
won't fit one bit because.
That. ain't. it.

~ Z.

A Message from the Mine

* * *

A bold new vision is what I've been praying for.

Practically slaving the day away,
day to day at my dead-beat 9 to 5 that had beaten me
mentally half to death.
I used to cry every time I had to go to work.

I hated being one of the "heroes"
in such a villainous world.
Not any sign of a name or number, but simply
an essential worker that was treated as a
common commodity.

Living in a pandemic, with my mind already in a
state of pandemonium wasn't even the worst part.
The worst part was that those around didn't seem to
notice or even care.
To them I was just… "hero."
I was no nurse or doctor. Just simply a patient sitter,
sitting in a mosh pit of her own emotions.

It was frowned upon to take mental health days, but I did it anyway.

Stuck in between a raging roommate and a series of crises where no resolution was to be seen, there I was. Alone, or so I thought.

Feeling unloved, ignored, and unwanted. I felt as though even my God had abandoned me.

I made some nice friends, but they eventually disappeared as well.

All is well in the well, beyond these hazel eyes laid an empty shell.

~ Z.

When Love Doubts Love

Fearfully and Wonderfully made in the image of God,
born with a name that quite literally means Gift from
God, Pure, and Keeper of Keys.

Yet I was still fearful of falling away into the
everlasting pit, far away from the very Being that
created and wrapped this gift.

Afraid that my works will be worthless and
that my existence will be in vain and
without meaning.

Afraid of a Being who can begin and end
the mist that is our lives, causing us to
vanish without a trace.

That isn't even the worst part.

The worst part is that He will answer
to no one for His actions.

Words with aggression ring throughout my head with
no discretion.

Words of disdain, doubtfulness, and accusations of
disloyalty from the enemy.
Whispers of treason and the penalties of such offense.
Yet my demise was not yet.

My demise came when the utterances of God's
disdain toward me came falling out of a dear friend's
mouth like waterfalls falling
off the edge of a cliff.
I died and was reborn that night.

Reborn into an empty, yet full version of myself.
Conceived in sorrow as I moaned and groaned with
grief over my current condition.
I cried my old soul out of existence, a new soul
forming within.

First came emptiness, then came fullness.
Fullness of joy, peace, and wisdom.
Carrying a fresh outlook on life,
I sang and danced again.

Here is wisdom, retain a loving fear of the
Lord and keep His commandments,
lest you fall to the same fate as I.

~ Z.

Born and Raised

* * *

I was born and raised in the bustling haze that is
Detroit city.

Sunny days teeming with the ever-so welcoming
aromas of family barbecues, things of which my
young mind carried with me.

Such things made my joy full.
Such things made me, joyful.
How unfortunate.

Many things of which became לבה as soon as I walked
into my broken home.

A broken home that brought me back to the realities
of my broken life.

There were no safe havens outside
of my mind then.

And so, I lived.

Lived inside my own imaginations
where nothing was impossible to me.

I lived freely, outside the binds of space and time.

But there I was, born and raised in the
bustling haze that is Detroit city.

~ Z.

Someone said
Something to Me Today

* * *

A man said something astonishing to me today.
To summarize, he said this:

"Sin is something Jesus handled already.
We as believers should be basing our decisions on
rather or not, they cause us to grow.
Not on the black and white scales of
'Is this a sin or not?'"

By this, he didn't say that we were
given a license to sin,
But rather that asking this question wasn't the place
to begin.
He said that we should merit or demerit our behavior
on whether or not this behavior
draws us closer to God and His high
calling on our lives.

That changed a lot for me you see.

A once dull religious experience is now a blossoming rainbow of excitement and curiosity.

No more boring lectures based on conjectures, or lessons deemed to display the miserable conditions that seem to lessen my chances at being in Heaven.

No. It meant more than that.

It meant that we ought to trust Christ's sacrifice and live lives according to the fullness of joy and the standard of holiness that we have been given.

Listening to that speech loosened satan's grip on me.

Cries of mourning in the dark of night turned to late night and early morning dancing.

With joyous midday singing.

It made my heart glad and my bones strong.

~ Z.

A Letter to All
the Peoples of the Earth

* * *

First, to the people who inspired the whole world,

Your inner beauty is only surpassed by that of the
Heavenly hosts and the Godhead Himself.

Yet you are being blamed for all the ugliness in the earth.

Please know that this is not all your fault,

for the devil has aroused the hatred that exists in this
world, and he uses his agents to complete his evil
works.

God loves you more than the very angels in Heaven,
even when what's happening around you tries to tell
you differently.

Next, to the peoples who are being taken for granted,

You are seen and heard by God who is enthroned in
Heaven,

One who is enthralled by you.

His affections and attention are on you always.

He is always concerned with you,
every part of your being.

From your inner most strangeness,
to your outer subtle novelty.

Speak to Him, for He is always listening and is eager
to converse and collaborate with you.

Last but certainly not least, to the peoples who are
counted among the least of those who walk the face
of the earth.

You may not have the fancy clothes, the so-called
"perfect body" or the newest car, house, and tech, but
allow me to share what you do have.

You have God's heart and His relatability.

Your sufferings are not vague to the Lord Jesus Christ
Himself. (Romans 8:3-4)

He Himself was homeless, but God has housed him
in Glory.

He was poor, yet the Father has given Him wealth
that surpasses any worldly dollar amount.

He was lonely, yet the Father and all of Heaven adores
Him and is in His company.

He was abused unjustly by the likes of evil people,
but God has used His sufferings for glory.

All of these things happened to Him for the sake of love. More specifically, for the sake of God's love for us all.

As with Him, so with you. (1 Peter 5:10)

God adores you, for all the earth and the peoples in it are His. (Psalm 24:1, Colossians 1:16-17)

God is exceedingly able to surpass all of your heart's desires and meet any and all of your needs.

Men have wronged you, but your Father in Heaven never will, for His Goodness stretches from everlasting to everlasting.

God has forever been a present help in trouble (Psalm 46:1), abounding in steadfast love, peace, patience, joy, kindness, goodness, and faithfulness. (Galatians 5:22).

Now to all the peoples of the earth,

God loves you so much that He sent His own Son to be tortured and die for you,

all of that pain so that you may be where He currently resides, in Heaven and in the future, the New Earth, for all of eternity. (John 3:16)

No being (physical or spiritual), situation, pain or strife, Heaven above, nor hell below can separate ANY of you from God's love. (Romans 8:38-39)

For you are fearfully and wonderfully made (Psalm 139:1-5), carefully woven into your mother's womb by the Creator of the deepest oceans, lowest valleys, tallest mountains, largest planets, brightest stars, even up to the entire universe and all that dwells both in and outside of time itself.

Shalom, God loves you and so do I.

"May the grace of the Lord Jesus Christ, the love of God, and the fellowship of the Holy Spirit be with you all."

~ Z.

About The Author

Zy'Kia Newby was born and raised in Detroit, Michigan. From the time she was young, she was always reading or writing something. She has hopes to do macro community work such as organizing social justice and awareness events. Her ultimate goal is always to glorify God with her life.